Countries and Cultures for Young Explorers
JAPAN

Written by
Lynita Strei

Inside Illustrations by
Roberta Collier-Morales

Cover Illustration by
Laura Zarrin

Published by Instructional Fair • TS Denison
an imprint of

 **McGraw-Hill
Children's Publishing**

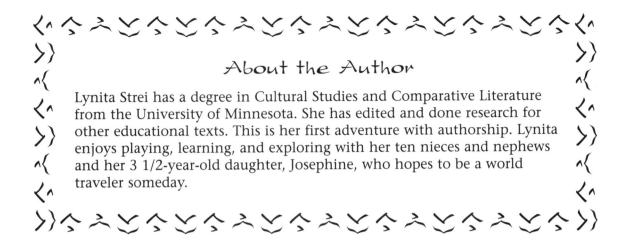

About the Author

Lynita Strei has a degree in Cultural Studies and Comparative Literature from the University of Minnesota. She has edited and done research for other educational texts. This is her first adventure with authorship. Lynita enjoys playing, learning, and exploring with her ten nieces and nephews and her 3 1/2-year-old daughter, Josephine, who hopes to be a world traveler someday.

Credits

Author: Lynita Strei
Illustrator: Roberta Collier-Morales
Cover Artist: Laura Zarrin
Cover Graphics: Peggy Jackson
Project Director/Editor: Sara Bierling
Editors: Kathryn Wheeler, Jane Haradine
Page Layout: Tracy L. Wesorick

McGraw-Hill
Children's Publishing

A Division of The McGraw·Hill Companies

Published by Instructional Fair • TS Denison
An imprint of McGraw-Hill Children's Publishing
Copyright © 2000 McGraw-Hill Children's Publishing

Send all inquiries to:
McGraw-Hill Children's Publishing
3195 Wilson Drive NW
Grand Rapids, Michigan 49544

Countries and Cultures for Young Explorers: Japan
ISBN: 0-7424-0032-8

Table of Contents

Introduction

Japan is a country rich in culture and beauty. Young students will explore this colorful and diverse land through activities and information intended to spark their imaginations.

A young resident of Japan named Keiko guides students along the journey by providing narratives from a child's point of view. Students will learn about Keiko's home, family, favorite meals, and past-times as they hear personal stories that vividly portray Japanese culture with fun and excitement. Sections narrated by Keiko are identified by a picture of Keiko near the beginning of each narrative. These stories provide background material for the activities, but may be long for reading aloud in single sittings. We suggest you read Keiko's information in parts, as needed or appropriate. Use your best judgment as to what will captivate your students' attention. Those sections not narrated by Keiko are best read by the teacher and their information given to students as needed.

Accompanying each narrative is a set of activities, varying from discussions to projects from which the teacher may choose. Many activities may be made easier to suit younger students.

Included are cross-curricular activities and projects, reproducible pages, and mini-books. These pages are designed to actively involve the students in learning about the culture of Japan. Many student worksheets apply directly to the activities presented in the teacher pages. Others are simply supplementary and may be completed by students on individual bases.

Students will begin the adventure through Japan with a reproducible flag and passport. The students may color the flag and fold the passport. To make passports more authentic, students may draw pictures of themselves or paste in photos.

A traveler's suitcase pattern is included at the back of the book to allow students to save the worksheets and projects they have completed. This will not only help students retain learned information but also remind them of the fun and adventure they experienced during their study of Japan.

Utilize the resource lists in the back of the book to enhance the journey with photographs of featured subjects, children's books about Japan, and educational Web sites.

Have fun with your adventures!

4

Japan

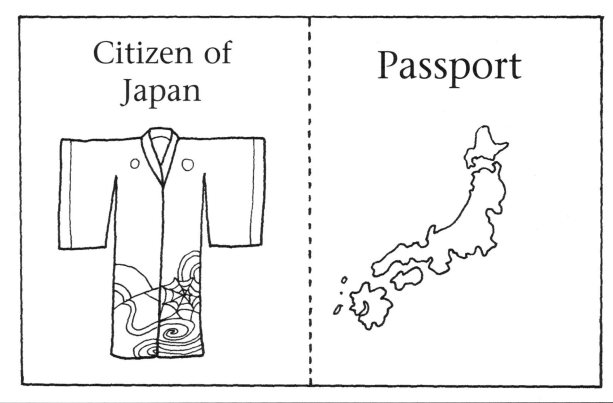

Citizen of Japan

Passport

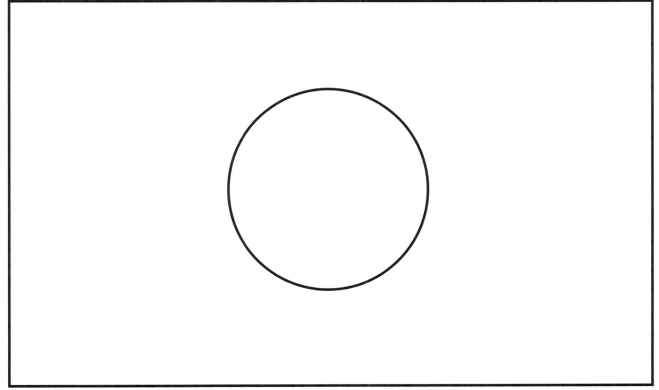

Konnichiwa!

Konnichiwa (koh-NEE-chee-wah)! That is how we say hello in Japanese. We always bow when we say hello to show respect. My name is Keiko, and I live in Tokyo, the largest city in Japan. We call Japan *Nippon*, which means "source of the sun" or "land of the rising sun."

Houses are hard to find in Tokyo because there are so many people living here. Some families have to wait for two years to get their own apartments. My father, mother, my older brother, and I live together. Our apartment has two traditional Japanese-style rooms, a kitchen, a bathroom, and one Western-style room with a couch, television, and chairs. Japanese-style rooms have very little furniture. *Tatami* (tah-TAH-mee) mats (these are used like carpeting) are on the floor during the day. At night we sleep on the floor on *futons* (FOO-tahns). Futons are thick, soft mattresses made of cotton. They are rolled up and stored during the day to save space.

Japanese rooms do not have any chairs. We eat at a very low table, sitting on pillows. We always take our shoes off before entering the house. *Shojii* (SHOH-jee) are paper screens that divide the rooms. They slide open and closed. Many Japanese houses have a *tokonoma* (toh-koh-NOH-mah). This is a small nook where there is a painting and a table with a floral arrangement.

Activity

Students may color and read the mini-books on pages 8 and 11. They may also complete the maze on page 9.

Activity

Make a tatami mat.

Materials:
   three colors of construction paper
   scissors
   glue

Directions:

1. Fold one piece of construction paper in half lengthwise. Cut strips about 1 inch (2.5 cm) apart, going from the fold toward the open edges of the paper. Be careful not to cut all the way through the paper.
2. Cut strips 1 inch (2.5 cm) wide from the other two colors of construction paper. Weave the strips of paper through the first paper. Alternate the colors. Glue in place.

Activity

Make a Japanese shoebox home. Ask the students to bring shoeboxes to school (or provide some for them). Have them decorate the insides of the shoeboxes to look like the insides of traditional Japanese rooms. What material will they use for the tatami floor coverings? Remember the low table.

Otosan and Okasan

My father, my *otosan* (oh-TOH-sahn), goes to work very early every morning and gets home very late every night. He works long hours at the factory where he is a supervisor. The factory makes stereos that are sold all over the world.

My mother, my *okasan* (oh-KAH-sahn), works very hard, too. She works as a teacher in my school. She also has to prepare all of our meals. There is not much room in our kitchen for storing food, so she must go shopping for fresh food every day.

Obaasan and Ojiisan

My grandparents live in the same house where my mother grew up. It is near a rice paddy. A rice paddy is a wet, swampy piece of land where rice is grown.

There are many rice paddies in Japan. My grandfather, my *ojiisan* (oh-JEE-ee-sahn), grew up on this same farm. When we go to visit, my ojiisan tells my brother and me stories of planting the rice by hand. My ojiisan is very proud to grow rice.

My grandmother, my *obaasan* (oh-BAH-sahn), always wears the traditional dress, called a *kimono* (kih-MOH-noh). This is a loose-fitting dress, like a robe. Each kimono is tied together with an *obi* (OH-bee), which is a sash. Kimonos are very beautiful, but I like to wear jeans and T-shirts most of the time. My obaasan would like my mother and me to wear kimonos all of the time.

Activity

Read these books to the class about Japanese village life: *Girl from the Snow Country* by Masako Hidaka, and *The Sea and I* by Harutaka Nakawatari.

Activity

Lead a discussion about grandparents. When students visit their grandparents, are things different than at home? Have students evaluate how their responses differ. Would students rather live in the city or in the country? Why?

Activity

To get an idea of what a traditional Japanese dress is like, make this spoon doll fitted with a traditional kimono.

Materials:
    plastic spoon (one for each student)
    black yarn
    wallpaper scraps (fairly large pieces, or
      use decorated construction paper)
    construction paper pieces in flesh tones
      and black (for hands and shoes)
    scissors
    glue
    black marker

Directions:

1. Draw a face onto the bowl of the spoon.
2. Cut the yarn for hair and glue onto the back of the spoon.
3. Fold a piece of wallpaper in half. Trace the pattern from page 10 and cut out, avoiding the top edge, but cutting out the notch.
4. Cut two feet and hands out of the construction paper from the patterns provided.
5. Place the spoon through the cut-out in the top of the kimono and glue to secure. Glue the hands and feet to the inside of the kimono.

Sensei Says

At 8:30 we start our school day with some exercises—the teachers too! It helps us to focus on our school work and not goofing around. We have classes in math, science, art, physical education, Japanese, and kanji. Kanji is what the Japanese characters are called. We learn to write them in a beautiful way. My *sensei* (SEHN-say) (teacher) says it is very important to learn to write the characters correctly.

Our school year is very long. We start in April and do not finish until the following March. We only get six weeks of vacation! Many kids go to another school at night, called *juku* (JOO-koo). This is a cramming school. At juku, students are tutored on how to pass exams. The exams are very difficult, and you have to pass in order to go to the next grade.

We have earthquake drills in our school. There is an earthquake at least once a day in Japan. Most of the time you do not notice them. But we have drills just in case there is a big one. There is an old story about why there are so many earthquakes in Japan. It is said that there is a giant catfish that lives under the islands, and when it swishes its tail, it causes another earthquake. This is a neat story, but in our geology class, we are learning the real reason for earthquakes.

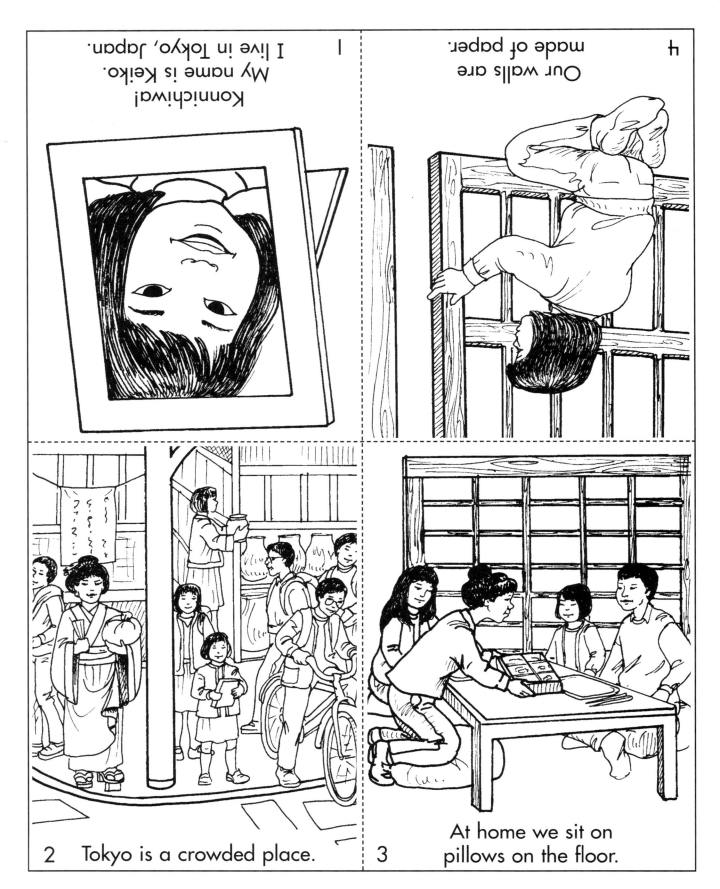

Konnichiwa! My name is Keiko. I live in Tokyo, Japan. 1

Our walls are made of paper. 4

2 Tokyo is a crowded place.

3 At home we sit on pillows on the floor.

Commuter Maze

Kimono Pattern

IF2631 *Countries and Cultures: Japan*

1 We start our day at school doing exercises.

4 My brother and I have lots of homework.

2 We learn to draw kanji characters.

3 After school I go to swimming lessons.

Speaking Japanese

Family

These are the terms used when speaking to one's own family or about someone else's.

otosan (oh-TOH-sahn)—father

okasan (oh-KAH-sahn)—mother

ojiisan (oh-JEE-ee-sahn)—grandfather

obaasan (oh-BAH-sahn)—grandmother

onesan (oh-NEH-sahn)—sister (older)

imotosan (ee-MOH-toh-sahn)—sister (younger)

onisan (oh-NEE-sahn)—brother (older)

ototosan (oh-TOH-toh-sahn)—brother (younger)

Greetings

konnichiwa (koh-NEE-chee-wah)—hello

ohayo gozaimasu (oh-HAH-yoh goh-ZAH-ee-mahs)—good morning

sayonara (sah-yoh-NAH-rah)—good-bye

domo arigato (DOH-moh ah-ree-GAH-toh)—thank you

sumimasen (soo-MEE-mah-sehn)—excuse me

onegai shimasu (oh-neh-GAH-ee shee-MAHS)—please

hai (HAH-ee)—yes

Iie (ee-EH)—no

Activity

Practice pronouncing and using these words by greeting your students in the morning with "ohayo gozaimasu." Have the students practice saying the words aloud—in groups and in front of the class. Have each student pick one or two of the family names to use at home.

Activity

Help students complete the decoding activity on page 14.

Names in Japan

In Japan, the family name comes before the first name. For example, Keiko's family name is Takahashi, so she is Takahashi Keiko. Girls' names usually end in *-ko*, which means "little" or "child."

Activity

Have each student write his or her name reversed, in the Japanese style. The girls could try adding *-ko* to the ends of their names.

Counting to Ten

ichi (EE-chee)—one

ni (NEE)—two

san (SAHN)—three

shi (SHEE)—four

go (GOH)—five

roku (ROH-koo)—six

shichi (SHEE-chee)—seven

hachi (HAH-chee)—eight

ku (KOO)—nine

ju (JOO)—ten

Activity

Practice pronouncing the numbers one through ten as a class. Have each student learn how to pronounce the number of his or her own age. The older students can learn to spell and pronounce the Japanese number of their own ages.

Activity

Reproduce the vocabulary cards on page 15 and hand out a set to each student. Have them color and cut. Have students drill each other using the cards.

Colors

ao (AH-oh)—blue

aka (AH-kah)—red

ki iro (KEE EE-roh)—yellow

midori iro (mi-DOH-ree EE-roh)—green

orenji iro (oh-REN-jee EE-roh)—orange

murasaki iro (moor-ah-SAH-kee EE-roh)— purple

shiro (SHEE-roh)—white

momoiro (moh-moh-EE-roh)—pink

kuro (KOO-roh)—black

chairo (chah-EE-roh)—brown

Activity

Have each child practice pronouncing the color of the shirt he or she is wearing.

Activity

Help students complete the coloring activity on page 16.

Speaking Without Words

The Japanese also have ways of communicating without words. Certain gestures or movements have meaning. Here are a few examples:

- A downward wave with one hand means "Come here."

- Holding your hands up above your head in a V shape and saying "Ganbare (gahn-bahr-AY)!" means "Hurrah!"

- To show that something is favorable or very good, make a circle with your arms.

- When saying "hello," "goodbye," "thank you," or "I'm sorry," the Japanese bow politely with their hands at their sides.

- When indicating oneself, the Japanese point to the nose, not the heart.

Activity

Try out these gestures and discuss how they are different from the ones used where you live. Do some students in the class use gestures that others don't? If necessary, explain why some gestures are inappropriate.

Kanji

Kanji characters are the written form of the Japanese language. The characters were adapted from those used in China. Kanji is complex and difficult to learn because there are great numbers of characters.

Activity

Explore the Internet for calligraphy examples. Do a search for "Japanese calligraphy" or "kanji" or go to these sites: *www.globalserve.net/~fylypchuk/kanji/ kanjiframe.html*. This has great examples of kanji characters. Just click on a character, and the meaning is listed.

www2.gol.com/users/billp/students/ kanjiname/nameindex.html includes a class project at a school in Japan. Click on a student's name, and it shows how to write it in kanji and explains the meaning of the name.

Activity

Students can practice writing kanji by tracing and then drawing the sample characters on page 17.

Decoding Activity

Use the code to find out what Keiko is saying. Then color the page.

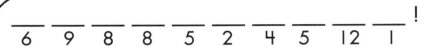

$$\overline{}_{6}\ \overline{}_{9}\ \overline{}_{8}\ \overline{}_{8}\ \overline{}_{5}\ \overline{}_{2}\ \overline{}_{4}\ \overline{}_{5}\ \overline{}_{12}\ \overline{}_{1}\ !$$

$$\overline{}_{9}\ \overline{}_{4}\ \overline{}_{1}\ \overline{}_{13}\ \overline{}_{9}$$

$$\overline{}_{3}\ \overline{}_{9}\ \overline{}_{14}\ \overline{}_{1}\ \overline{}_{5}\ \overline{}_{7}\ \overline{}_{1}\ \overline{}_{10}\ \overline{}_{11}$$

A–1
C–2
G–3
H–4
I–5
K–6
M–7
N–8
O–9
S–10
U–11
W–12
Y–13
Z–14

14

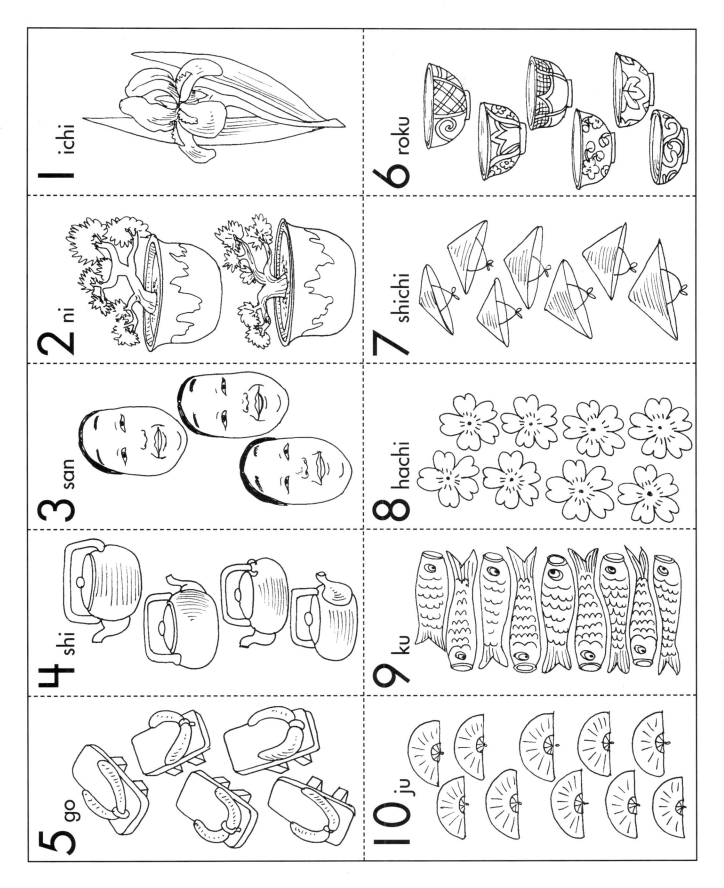

1 ichi

2 ni

3 san

4 shi

5 go

6 roku

7 shichi

8 hachi

9 ku

10 ju

IF2631 *Countries and Cultures: Japan*

Coloring Japan

blue=ao   green=midori iro   black=kuro   yellow=ki iro

pink=momoiro   orange=orenji iro   purple=murasaki iro

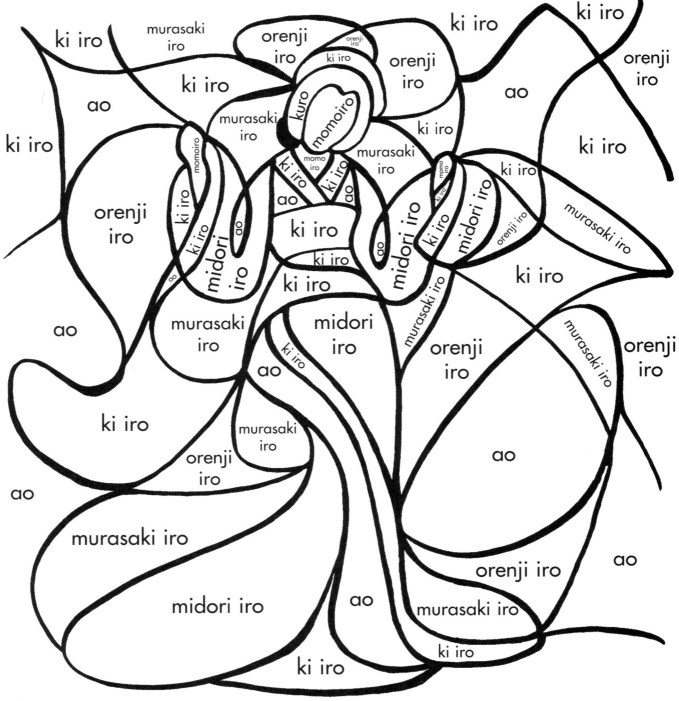

Kanji Calligraphy

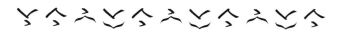

Trace these characters. Older students may be able to draw them on their own.

This character means "sun":

This character means "tree":

Trace   *Practice*

_____

_____

Fun in Japan

Besuboru

In Japan, we call baseball *yakyu* (YAH-que). Sometimes we call it *besuboru* (bay-soo-BOH-roo), which sounds more like the American word. It seems like everyone in Japan is crazy for it. My brother used to dream about playing professional yakyu, but now his schoolwork takes up too much of his time. His favorite team is the Tokyo Giants. My father likes to take us to the Tokyo Dome to watch their games. Almost every city in Japan has its own team. Even high school games are shown on television because so many people like to watch besuboru.

Activity

"*Puure booru* (Play ball)!" Play a game of baseball, the favorite sport of Japan. Divide the class into two teams. Look at a map of Japan and have each team pick a city in Japan for which they can pretend to be playing. Then have them come up with names for their teams. (In Japan, team names are similar to those of American teams. For example, there are teams in Japan called the Tokyo Giants, Seibu Lions, and the Kintetsu Buffaloes.) Then have fun playing the game. It may be easier to play your baseball game inside a gymnasium using a soft ball and a plastic bat. Adjust your game for the age level you are instructing.

Sumo and the Martial Arts

Have you ever seen two 136-kilogram (300-lb.) men, wearing almost nothing, rush into each other while grunting and snorting? In Japan this is part of an ancient tradition. *Sumo* (SOO-moh) wrestling is the national sport of Japan. This sport is practiced only in Japan. There are six major sumo tournaments a year, and many people go to see them. It takes great skill to win a match. Most sumo matches last only about thirty seconds. If any part of a wrestler's body except his feet touches the ground, he loses. Sumo wrestlers have to eat special food to gain weight. Do not let their size fool you; sumo wrestlers are very powerful and skillful.

Sumo wrestling comes from the ancient samurai warriors. *Samurai* (SAH-moo-rahee) warriors were brave and honored fighters in Japanese history. Other methods of fighting also come from the samurais, including karate, kendo, judo, and aikido. These are all forms of fighting called "martial arts." Each of these martial arts is very different. What makes them special to us is how they combine body strength with inner strength. This means that it is not just how hard you hit or how big and strong you are but how well you can control your mind over your body.

Activity

How many children in your classroom would it take to equal one 300-pound (136-kg) sumo wrestler? Figure it out!

Activity

Ask the students if any of them are involved in the martial arts. Do they feel it is both physical and spiritual? Ask them to demonstrate some moves (safely, of course). Or, ask students if they have seen any movies or read any books that show the martial arts. Would they ever want to try one of the martial arts?

Pachinko

Say the word *pachinko* (pah-CHEEN-koh) three times really fast. Does it sound kind of like the noise a pinball machine makes? My father loves pachinko. It is like American pinball, but the machines are attached to a wall. My mother says it is a waste of time and money. There are arcades all over Japan where the walls are lined with pachinko games. Businessmen line up to use them after work. My brother and I prefer playing computer games.

Activity

Help students complete the Sports Scramble page. They may need assistance with the challenging words. Students may also color and read the mini-book on page 21.

Activity

Play *Kai-awase* (kai–ah-WAH-see). This game was originally made from the two parts of a bivalve shell that were beautifully painted with scenes from nature or everyday life. The halves of each shell were split apart and put with others on a table. The object was to match the two halves again. (This game is very much like other memory games.)

Materials:
    white tag board
    scissors
    markers or crayons
    stickers (optional)

Directions:

1. Make 20 shells of identical shape by using a pattern traced onto tag board.
2. Use markers to decorate them, producing 10 identical pairs. Optional: To save time, you may use 10 pairs of stickers.

To Play:

1. Shuffle the shells. Turn the shells design side down on a table. Arrange them in three circles of 4, 6, and 10 shells (see diagram).
2. Each player turns over two shells, looking for a match. If a match is made, the player takes another turn. If not, the next player gets a turn.
3. The player with the most pairs is the winner.

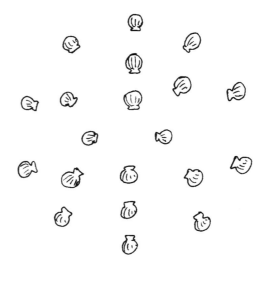

Sports Scramble

Unscramble these words about sports in Japan.

1. abll _____

2. mwis  _____

3. orspts  _____

4. sgmea  _____

Challenging Words

5. ousm  _____

6. ujdo _____

7. esbbllaa _____

(Answers: 1. ball, 2. swim, 3. sports, 4. games, 5. sumo, 6. judo, 7. baseball)

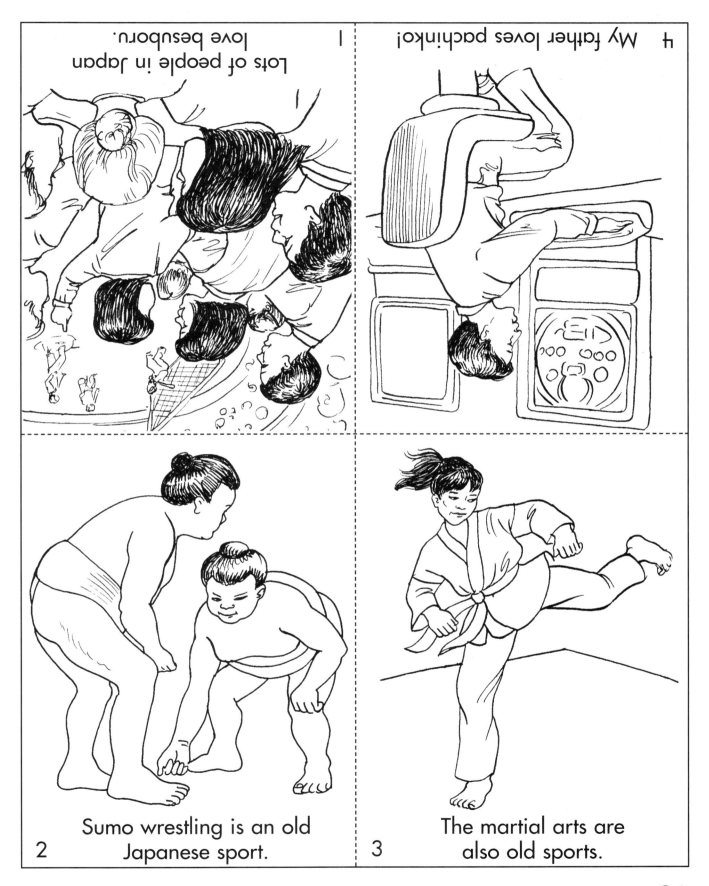

1   Lots of people in Japan love besuboru.

4   My father loves pachinko!

2   Sumo wrestling is an old Japanese sport.

3   The martial arts are also old sports.

IF2631 Countries and Cultures: Japan

Japanese Festivals

New Year

The biggest celebration in Japan is for New Year. We call it *Shogatsu* (shoh-GAHT-soo). We prepare for the coming of the new year by cleaning the entire house.  This gives everything a clean start. All debts are paid, and if you and a friend or family member have a disagreement, it is always best to resolve it before the new year begins. It would be bad luck for the whole year if we do not take care of these things by December 31. Then we place pine branches and bamboo stalks outside the house. Pine branches symbolize a long, healthy life, as well as faithfulness. We use bamboo stalks to symbolize strength and flexibility. On the stroke of midnight, each Japanese temple rings a bell 108 times. Then my brother and I open red envelopes with gifts of money inside!

Activity

Celebrate Shogatsu in your classroom. During the time before the New Year, have the students help you clean the classroom. (You can encourage them by telling them that Japanese students are usually responsible for cleaning the school, just as the janitor does.) Decorate the room with pine branches and—if you can get them—bamboo stalks and straw ropes. An alternative could be to serve your students sliced bamboo shoots as a snack (these come canned and are readily available in the oriental food section of most supermarkets). In lieu of giving students gifts of money, have classmates write notes of encouragement sealed in red paper or envelopes. Each student will get one red envelope to open.

Children's Day

On May 5, Japanese children have their own holiday! It is called Children's Day. Every family with children hangs up fish-shaped streamers on a bamboo pole outside the house. The fish are carp, which represent strength and good luck. One fish is flown for each child in the family. The largest fish represents the oldest child of the family. It is neat to see fish swinging in the wind all over Tokyo that day! We eat special treats and celebrate all day. This day reminds us of how important we are to our families.

Activity

Use the pattern on page 24 to have each student make his or her own fish wind sock out of a brown lunch bag. To display the wind socks, either hang them from the ceiling, or, if possible, tie them to a flagpole outside the school.

Materials:
    two copies of fish pattern for each
        student
    markers or paints
    string
    paper hole reinforcers
    brown paper lunch bag

Directions:

1. Cut out the bottom of the lunch bags. (This probably should be done before giving them to the students.)
2. Give each student two copies of the fish pattern and have them color and decorate them.
3. Have the students cut out and paste the fish, one on each side, to the lunch bag.

4. Punch four holes in the top of the bag, two holes on each long side. Attach the reinforcers.

5. Run strings through the holes, then tie all the strings together. Hang.

Cherry Blossom Festival

In Japan, nature and its beauty are special to us. The Cherry Blossom Festival is held every spring. *Ueno* (oo-EH-noh) Park in Tokyo is an amazing sight, blazing with pink cherry blossoms. We always go to the park very early in the day to find a place to sit. There are as many people crammed into the park as there are cherry blossoms. It is worth it to see the beautiful trees and smell the sweet blossoms. We eat cherry candies and make cherry blossom tea. I wear my kimono that is decorated with cherry blossom designs.

Activity

Make paper cherry blossoms. This project is simple and each student can create his or her own cherry blossoms. They may decorate their desks, or the blossoms can be strung together to form a chain to decorate the classroom. This activity could be done during the festival (see Matsuri section) or in preparation for it.

Materials:
    pieces of tissue paper or construction paper cut into 4-inch (10-cm) squares
    3-inch (7 1/2-cm) pieces of drinking straws, one for each blossom
    string
    paper punch

Directions:

1. Fold a 4-inch (10-cm) square piece of paper as shown in the diagrams and cut.

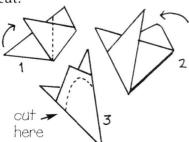

2. Cut one long piece of string, allowing approximately 18 inches (46 cm) per child in the class. Punch holes in the flowers and string them, alternating with a piece of the straw.

Activity

Help students learn the song *Sakura*, on page 25. If possible, perform it for the whole school during an assembly that presents your study of Japan.

Classroom Matsuri

Set aside a special day for a Japanese festival (*matsuri* [maht-SOO-ree]). When the students arrive on festival day, have them take their shoes off before entering the room. The shoes should be neatly lined up outside the door, according to Japanese tradition. Play some traditional Japanese folk music.

If possible, find low tables at which the students can sit. Sturdy cardboard boxes or coffee tables would work well. The students should sit on the floor on pillows and use a place mat or napkin to put at their spot on the table. Before festival day, have the students create Japanese-looking place mats and have the place mats laminated. Students may then take the mats home as keepsakes.

On many Japanese holidays, the children are served rice cakes, some of them sweetened. Have one or two students serve their classmates rice cakes. They should bow when being served and say the Japanese words for "thank you," *domo arigato* (DOH-moh ah-ree-GAH-toh).

Try some of the recipes in the food section and bring chopsticks for the students to try.

Fish Pattern

IF2631 *Countries and Cultures: Japan*

Sakura
(Cherry Trees)

This is a traditional Japanese song celebrating the cherry blossoms' beauty. Try the English and the Japanese versions during your matsuri.

Sa - ku - ra! Sa - ku - ra! Ya - ya - i no so - ra
Cher- ry trees, cher - ry trees, Bloom so bright in A - pril

wa, Mi - wa - ta - su ka - ghi ri; Ka - su - mi ka?
breeze. Like a mist or float - ing cloud; Fra - grance fills the

Ku - mo - ka? Ni - o - i zo i - zu - ru;
air a - round, Shad - ows flit a - long the ground.

I - za ya! I - za ya! Mi - ni yu - ka - n.
Come, oh, come! Come, oh, come! Come, see cher - ry trees!

 IF2631 *Countries and Cultures: Japan*

Rice, Tea, and Chopsticks

The word for "meal" in Japanese is *gohan* (GOH-hahn), which means "rice." Rice is served at every meal. Breakfast is called "morning rice," or in Japanese *asa-gohan* (AH-sah–GOH-han), lunch is "noon rice," *hiru-gohan* (HEE-roo–GOH-hahn), and supper is "evening rice," or *yuu-gohan* (YOO-oo–GOH-hahn). I have heard that in America, every house has a microwave. Well, in Japan, every house has an electric pot called a "rice cooker."

Another thing found in every house in Japan is a teapot. We call tea *ocha* (oh-CHAH). We have green tea at most meals, but I also like to drink cola when we have it in the house. We do eat lots of other things besides rice. Sometimes we have eggs and toast or omelettes. *Tempura* (tem-POO-rah) is one of my favorite foods for dinner. This is battered and fried vegetables, sometimes made with chicken or beef, but always served with gohan. *Sashami* (sah-SHAH-mee) is raw fish that we dip in *wasabi* (wah-SAH-bee), a spicy sauce. We eat lots of fish, but we also eat seaweed. We eat it dried or fresh. *Sushi* (SOO-shee) is rice with vinegar rolled up in seaweed. It is usually stuffed with cucumbers or raw fish. We dip sushi in soy sauce. It is delicious!

We eat our food with chopsticks. Chopsticks are long, cylindrical sticks that are pointed on one end. Chopsticks take a while to get used to using. Can you guess how we eat soup without spoons? We pick out the big pieces with our chopsticks and then pick up the bowl and drink the broth. Slurping is not rude in Japan; it is considered a compliment!

The preparation of food in Japan is considered an art form. My mother takes a lot of time to prepare our meals. Each day she makes everyone in the family an *o-bento* (oh–BEHN-toh), or lunch box, to take to school or work. An o-bento is a rectangular box with small compartments inside. My mother carefully fills each section with sushi, dried seaweed, pickled salmon, and apples that she cuts into shapes to look like different animals. My favorite shape is the rabbit.

Activity

For fun, serve your students noodle soup. This can be prepared easily by combining cooked spaghetti with your choice of hot broth (vegetable broth is a healthy choice). Spoon the soup into bowls, (usually there are more noodles than broth). Have students eat as many noodles as they can with chopsticks. Then let them slurp up the broth. They'll have great fun making the slurping noises. Make sure to keep plenty of napkins on hand!

Chopstick Challenge

How to use chopsticks:

Hold the chopsticks in your right hand (left hand for "lefties"). The thicker end is the end to hold on to; the pointed end is for the food.

The lower chopstick should be held steady at the base of the thumb, supported by the middle and ring fingers.

The upper chopstick is held between the thumb and index finger (like a pencil). It is moved to pick up food while the lower chopstick stays in place.

It is considered very rude to "spear" food with the pointy ends of the chopsticks. It is also rude to point at people with them or lick food off them. Holding chopsticks with your fist looks as if they are being used as a weapon and is not considered good manners. Never stick chopsticks straight up into a bowl of rice. This is a sign of mourning for the dead and should not be done at a meal. To dish food out of a serving bowl, use the thick end of the chopsticks that have not been in your mouth.

Activity

Take the chopstick challenge. If real chopsticks are not available, try using two pencils and have the students attempt to pick up crunched-up pieces of paper.

Activity

Read a book to the class about Japanese food or eating. Suggestions are *Yoko* by Rosemary Wells, *How My Parents Learned to Eat* by Ina R. Friedman, and *Everybody Cooks Rice* by Norah Dooley.

Activity

Have students fill in the compartments of the o-bento on page 31 with the foods they would like to have for lunch by drawing each food item. Have them share why they chose particular foods and if they think they have made good choices.

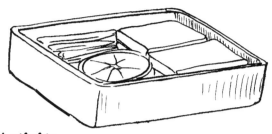

Activity

Serve your students tea. You may use green tea to be accurate or choose a fruit or herbal tea that might appeal more to the tastes of young ones. If you choose to serve strong tea, you may wish to add sugar to it before serving.

© Instructional Fair • TS Denison

Omelettes with Peas

Omelettes are popular in Japan for breakfast or lunch. They can be served hot or cold and are usually sliced into small rolls. Keiko's mother packs the slices into Keiko's o-bento.

Ingredients:

3 eggs
1/4 (60 ml) cup broth
1 tsp. (5 ml) sugar
1 tbs. (15 ml) light soy sauce
1 tbs. (15 ml) peas
oil

Directions:

1. Crack the eggs into a bowl and add the broth, sugar, and soy sauce. Whisk or mix well with a fork.
2. Add the peas to the egg mixture.
3. Heat oil in a skillet at a medium temperature. When hot, pour the egg mixture in and cook until the eggs set.
4. Push from one end to the other using a spatula. Repeat until all the mixture is solid.
5. To shape the omelette into a roll, place on aluminum foil and roll up. Let set for about one minute.
6. Cut the omelette into 3/4-inch (2-cm) slices. Serve hot or cold.

Japanese Rice

Ingredients:

2 1/2 cups (600 ml) short-grain rice
3 cups (.7 L) water
water to rinse

Directions:

1. Put the rice in a pot and add water to stir and rinse. Drain and repeat the process three times, or until the water runs clear.
2. Add the 3 cups of water and allow to soak for 45 minutes.
3. Cook on medium-low heat for 10 minutes, gradually bringing to a vigorous boil.
4. Reduce the heat slightly and continue cooking for 5 minutes. Reduce heat again and simmer for 15 minutes.
5. Turn heat to high to evaporate any excess water. Remove from heat. Cover and let steam for 10 minutes.
6. Remove the lid quickly to prevent any excess water from dripping onto the rice. Use a wet wooden spatula or spoon to lightly mix the rice in a folding motion, so that the rice is fluffy.
7. Dish into individual bowls and eat with chopsticks.

Tea Cookies and Ice Cream

Ice Cream Ingredients:

macha (green tea powder)
1 container vanilla ice cream
fresh strawberries

Directions:

1. Allow the container of ice cream to soften and mix in the green tea powder to taste. (Be careful! This powder can be quite strong. Macha has a very high caffeine content; be careful that this doesn't conflict with any student's diet.)
2. Put the ice cream back in the freezer and let it freeze again before using. This is delicious served with fresh strawberries.

You can find a powdered green tea called "macha" used for the tea ceremony in any Japanese grocery. Other options may be to grind green tea leaves into a powder or steep a concentrated pot of green tea.

Cookie Ingredients:

macha
powdered shortbread mix

Directions:

1. Mix the macha into prepared shortbread mix. You may have to experiment with the amount. The cookies should have a beautiful green color and a pronounced flavor without being too strong.
2. Complete shortbread recipe as directed.

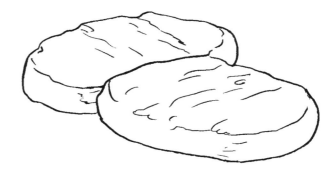

O-bento Activity

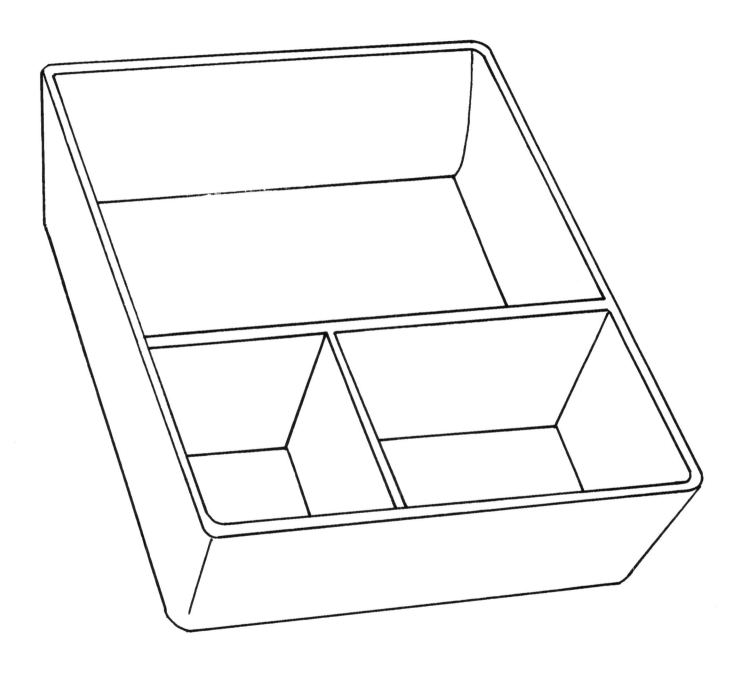

Japanese Arts

The Japanese consider many activities to be art forms: cooking, flower arranging, gardening, martial arts, even sumo wrestling. But there are master artists in painting, writing, and theater, too. The subjects that usually appear in paintings are nature, folktales, and actors in scenes from plays. Many paintings include calligraphy of Japanese kanji characters. Some of the most popular paintings in Japan are scrolls, long paper strips with kanji characters painted in black ink. Paintings are also done on screens used as room dividers to decorate homes.

Woodcut paintings became popular in Japan many hundreds of years ago. A picture is carved out of a block of wood. Then paint is applied to the wood and it is pressed onto paper.

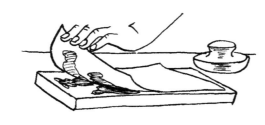

Activity

If possible, find and read *The Tale of the Mandarin Ducks* by Katherine Paterson. This book has illustrations done in the Japanese woodcut printing tradition.

Activity

In the tradition of Japanese woodcuts, do potato-cut prints instead.

Use raw, clean potatoes cut in half. Students can draw a picture on the flat surface of the potato with a pencil. Have the students choose a picture with a Japanese theme (for example, a cherry blossom or other flower, a fish, a kimono shape, or a rising sun). Next, students should cut the picture into the potato by cutting away the potato so the drawn picture is left. (You may wish to assist students with this step.) They then press the potato into paint or ink (or use a paint-soaked sponge to reduce dripping) and press onto paper.

Paper Folding

Origami (or-i-GAH-mee) is a form of Japanese art that involves paper folding. Origami means "folded paper." Most origami figures depict articles of nature, such as birds, flowers, and fish. The preferred paper for origami is a thin Japanese paper called *washi* (WAH-shee). Other papers are used as well. The most common sizes of paper squares used are 6 or 10 inches (15 or 25 cm).

Fans are important to Japanese culture. The ancient Japanese used fans in religious ceremonies. Warriors, rulers, and actors also used fans. They are often given as gifts.

Activity

Make origami cranes using the instructions on page 34.

Activity

Read *Sadako and the Thousand Paper Cranes* by Eleanor Coerr, a true story about a little Japanese girl. Or read *Tree of Cranes* by Allen Say. This story is about a Japanese boy's first Christmas.

Activity

Make a rigid fan. (You may also simply wish to have students decorate a piece of paper and then fold it accordion-style to create a fan.)

Materials:

    pattern on page 35
    glue
    tag board or lightweight cardboard
    markers
    lightweight paint-stirring or craft stick
    masking tape

Directions:

1. Photocopy the pattern. Have students color and cut out the fan.
2. They can glue the fan to tag board for stability and cut around the shape.
3. Students then glue the handle in place about halfway up the back of the fan.
4. Wrap the handle with masking tape.

Literature

Poems are fun to write. *Haiku* (hi-KOO) poems were first written in Japan and are now popular everywhere. Like many things in Japan, haiku poems are usually about nature. Haiku are short three-line poems. The first line has five syllables, the second has seven, and the third line has five syllables, again. Here is an example of a haiku poem by one of the greatest poets in Japan, Matsuo Basho (1644-1694). (Keep in mind that when translated into English, this haiku loses its standard syllabic form.)

A banana plant in the autumn gale—

I listen to the dripping of rain

Into a basin at night.

Activity

If it is age-appropriate, have students write their own haiku and present it on the haiku stationery on page 36.

Kabuki and Bunraku

One type of theater that began in Japan three hundred years ago is called *Kabuki* (kuh-BOO-kee). In this theater, the actors are all men. Even the female roles are played by men! They dress up in fancy costumes and wear lots of makeup. Their faces are white with painted eyes and mouths. These plays have sword fights,

samurais, music, and dancing.

Bunraku (boon-RAH-koo) theater is always fun. This is a kind of puppet theater. The wooden puppets used are almost four feet high. Each puppet needs three men to move it. Some of the puppets even move their mouths and eyebrows! The music at a Bunraku performance is made with a three-stringed instrument called a *samisen* (SAM-uh-sehn). The story in Bunraku is told by a narrator who uses different voices for different characters. The stories are usually folktales or traditional stories from Japan. The words are half-spoken and half-sung in the traditional way.

The costumes in Bunraku and Kabuki theater are all traditional Japanese styles. They wear kimonos and obis with one-strap sandals. The costumes are very colorful with lots of makeup and jewelry.

Activity

Explore Kabuki on the Internet. This Web site was designed by a Kabuki actor who still performs in Japan: *www.fix.co.jp/ kabuki/kabuki.html*. See step by step how the Kabuki actors put on makeup. Hear the sounds of the traditional music used in Kabuki plays, and hear the actors' calls. It also contains an online theater and a history of Kabuki theater.

Music

Most traditional Japanese music features a single melodic line, rather than a harmony. All of the voices of instruments involved play one melody. Traditional music features drums, flutes, gongs, and the samisen. Western music is also popular in Japan, and many cities have professional symphonies.

Activity

Have children learn the *Sakura* song on page 25 of the Japanese festivals section or the *Aizu Lullaby* on page 37.

33

Peace Crane

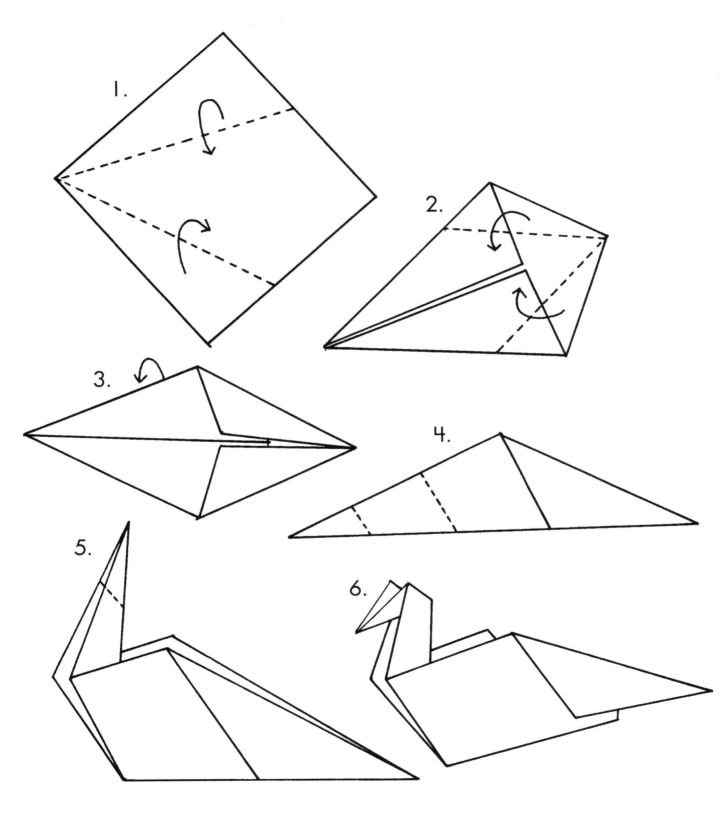

IF2631 *Countries and Cultures: Japan*

Rigid Fan Pattern

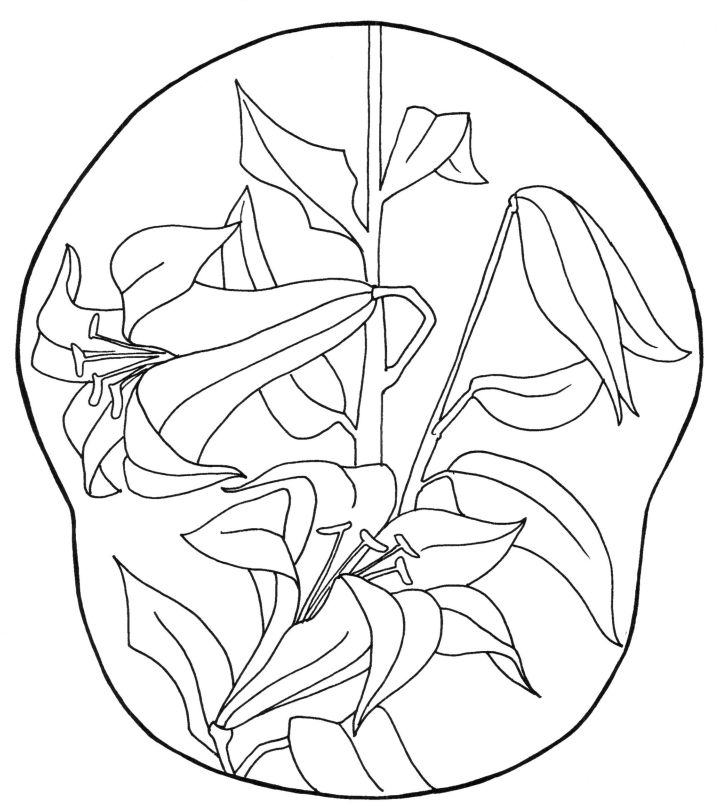

IF2631 *Countries and Cultures: Japan*

Aizu Lullaby

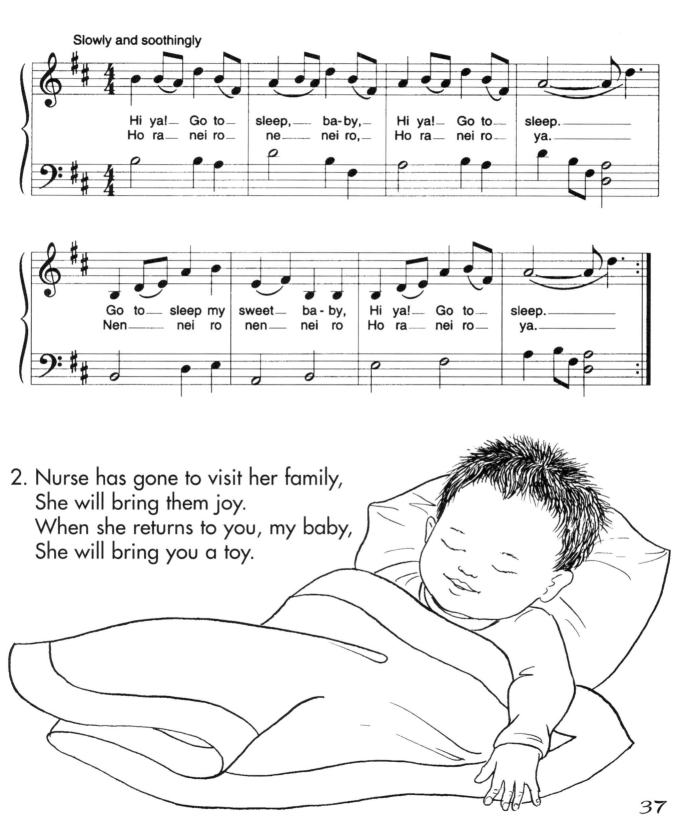

Slowly and soothingly

Hi ya! Go to sleep, ba-by, Hi ya! Go to sleep.
Ho ra nei ro ne nei ro, Ho ra nei ro ya.

Go to sleep my sweet ba-by, Hi ya! Go to sleep.
Nen nei ro nen nei ro Ho ra nei ro ya.

2. Nurse has gone to visit her family,
   She will bring them joy.
   When she returns to you, my baby,
   She will bring you a toy.

IF2631 *Countries and Cultures: Japan*

Temples and Shrines

Shinto

A tree, the wind, a rock, an ocean wave—what do they all have in common? *Kami* (KAH-mee), or divine spirits. All of these things are very important to us in a spiritual way. The word *shinto* (SHIN-toh) means "way of the gods." A shrine is a place where we go to pray and worship. A Shinto shrine always has a large gateway where we enter, called a *torii* (TOH-ree). There is also a place where we wash our hands and mouths in preparation for prayer. After washing, we bow twice, clap our hands together two times to get the gods' attention, and then bow again.

One of the ways to pray at a Shinto shrine is by leaving a strip of paper with a prayer tied to a sacred place within the shrine. Sometimes there are hundreds of little strips of paper tied to a tree or gate. Sometimes we bring fruit or coins and leave them as an offering.

Activity

Make a classroom torii. Use the design on page 40 to cut the shape out of tag board. Make the torii as large as possible. Secure it to a wall in the classroom or around a door, and decorate or paint it. In many cases, a torii has straw ropes tied between the two vertical poles. Simulate this if possible. Then have each student write a goal they have for their class or their school on a small strip of white paper and attach it to the gate. Remove one goal each day and read aloud to the class.

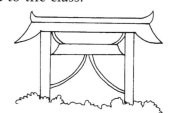

Buddhism

We once visited a city in Japan called Nara. We saw the largest statue I've ever seen. It is about 13 meters (42 ft.) tall! The statue is of *Buddha* (BOO-dah), a great religious teacher who lived thousands of years ago. Statues of Buddha usually show him meditating. The Nara statue is the largest bronze statue in the world.

I think the most important thing that Buddha has taught me is that happiness comes from wisdom and being a good person, not from money and expensive things.

The tea ceremony is a sacred ritual that came from Buddhism. It is called *chanoyu* (chah-NOH-yoo). My grandmother says it is a time to appreciate quietness, nature, friendship, and relaxation. The person serving the tea does it in a very special way. They have to know when and how to bow correctly and how to make the tea. There are strict rules for each part of the ceremony—even what to wear.

Activity

Look in an encyclopedia or reference book to find pictures of Buddha. Search the Internet for "buddhist temples" to find out what they look like.

Activity

Have your own chanoyu, or tea ceremony. Bring tea to the classroom and try to serve it in the traditional way. See if the students can practice this simplified method and not miss a step.

The traditional chanoyu uses tea cups with

no handles. Green tea is mixed with boiling water and then whisked to a froth. The tea is poured into the cup and passed to the receiver who bows and takes the cup with the right hand. The cup is then placed in the left hand and turned clockwise three times. The receiver takes a sip and wipes the cup with a cloth where the mouth touched it. Then the cup is passed to the next person.

Nature's Spirit in Japan

Nature is very important to the Japanese. Our gardens are designed to appreciate nature and quiet.

We do not have room for a garden in Tokyo. My father grows *bonsai* (BOHN-zai). Bonsai are miniature trees. They are shaped and tied down as they grow. The trees can be tiny and grown in a small pot, or they can be trimmed and shaped into plants the size of bushes. It takes a long time to learn how to grow bonsai trees the right way. The trees can last for many generations if they are grown correctly. My father still has a bonsai tree my grandfather gave him as a boy.

Rock formations, trees, and ponds become the centers of our gardens. One of my favorite places to go is along the ocean shore at Ise. There is a landform called the "wedded rocks." They are two large rocks sticking out of the water. There is an ancient myth that says these two rocks gave birth to the islands of Japan. Shinto priests tied thick rope from one rock to the other, like a bridge.

Simple, quiet, natural things are respected in the Buddhist religion, so that is how those gardens are made. Rocks, moss, ferns, and ponds with stepping-stones are carefully placed. There might be lanterns and bridges leading to a teahouse in the middle of the garden where the tea ceremony is performed.

Some of the most famous gardens in Japan are made by *Zen Buddhists*. Zen Buddhists study and meditate most of their lives. The gardens they create have no plants, trees, or water. They are made from only rocks and sand or gravel. They arrange rocks in different sizes and shapes and then rake sand or gravel around them in different patterns. The sand can be raked to look like water or the clouds and sky.

Activity

Search the Internet for pictures of Japanese gardens. Start by looking at *www.japanese-gardens-assoc.org*, which contains pictures and descriptions of Japanese gardens in the United States and in Japan.

Activity

Read *The Girl Who Loved Caterpillars: A Twelfth Century Tale from Japan* by Jean Merrill to the class. This book is about the Japanese appreciation for nature.

Activity

Design your own Zen garden. Give each student (or have them bring in) a shoebox. Put some fine sand in the bottom—about 2 inches deep. Then give students rocks of different sizes and shapes. Have them place the rocks in a design and then give them tools to rake the sand. Sandbox tools, forks, combs, or other kitchen utensils will work well. See if the students can make the sand look like waves or pond ripples.

Activity

Students may color and read the mini-book on page 41.

Torii Pattern

1 My father grows bonsai trees.

4 Zen gardens are simple rocks and sand.

2 We visit the sacred "wedded rocks."

3 Tea ceremonies are held in Buddhist gardens.

41

History and Geography

Shoguns and Samurai

Hundreds of years ago, military leaders, called *shoguns* (SHOH-guhnz), ruled Japan. The shogun was very powerful and had many people who served him. There were many poor people in Japan then, and they tried to fight against the shogun. Wars and uprisings occurred. The shogun needed warriors who could protect and fight for him. Trained fighters, called *samurai* (SAH-moo-rahee), were very brave warriors who would do anything for their shogun. (They were like medieval knights.) Samurai warriors were feared and respected throughout Japan.

The samurai wore two swords, one at each hip. These swords—one short and one long—were deadly and used whenever necessary. Samurai learned the "Way of the Warrior" or *bushido* (boo-SHEE-doh). They became masters with their swords and other weapons. Samurai wore armored coverings on their legs, chests, and arms, along with metal helmets. Their fighting skills were passed down from generation to generation. These skills, called "martial arts," are still practiced today in Japan and all over the world.

Activity

Students may complete the maze on page 44.

Tokyo or Edo

Tokyo was once called Edo. The city was the capital of Japan during the rule of the Tokugama shogun. The busy city streets of Edo were lined with teahouses; Kabuki theaters; shops and markets; and tightly packed rowhouses.

The shogun, his family, and many servants lived in the secluded Edo Castle, surrounded by a moat. They quietly wrote poetry or practiced other artistic crafts while safely protected from any outside harm.

The shogun wanted to be sure of his power. He not only barricaded the capital city, but all of Japan. During the rule of the Tokugawa shogun, the entire country of Japan was blocked from the rest of the world. No one was allowed to leave the country (or if they left, could not return), and no foreigners were allowed to enter. This lasted for about 200 years.

Activity

To explore the city of Edo and get a guided tour along the Tokaido, the main road to the city of Kyoto, visit this Internet site: *www.us-japan.org/edomatsu*. It has beautifully drawn storyboarded images of ancient Edo. It includes descriptions and narratives with information and educational links to other sites about Japan. Also included are pictures of samurai, shoguns, and villagers. Tour Edo Castle.

Activity

Invite a martial arts expert to demonstrate fighting skills and explain the philosophy of the martial arts to the class.

Activity

Read some Japanese folktales that involve samurai warriors or relate to the Edo period in Japanese history. Suggestions are *Little Fingerling: A Japanese Folktale* by Monica Hughes and *The Tale of the Mandarin Ducks* by Katherine Paterson.

Source of the Sun

Japan is made up of four big islands and about 3,900 smaller islands. If you were to sew all of the islands together into one piece of land, like a quilt, it would be about the size of the state of Montana in the United States. Japan has about half the population of the United States. It is a crowded country with about 126 million people.

Japan is surrounded by the Sea of Japan to the west and the Pacific Ocean to the east. One is never more than 100 miles (161 km) from water anywhere in Japan.

The four largest islands are called Honshu, Hokkaido, Kyushu, and Shikoku. Honshu is the biggest. The island chain makes a half-moon shape.

Japan is very mountainous, leaving even less living space for people. But the rugged peaks make Japan a beautiful and inspiring place. Mount Fuji, the tallest peak, rises 12,388 feet (3,776 m). It has been drawn, painted, and written about all through Japan's history. The Japanese call it *Fuji-san* (FOO-jee–sahn) or *Fujiyama* (foo-jee-YAH-mah). Thousands of people climb to the peak each year. When at the top, they pray at a sacred shrine.

Mount Fuji is an inactive volcano. There are many volcanoes in Japan. Although volcanoes can cause destruction, the hot rumbling earth also heats up water that makes steamy hot springs. The Japanese visit these on their holidays.

Activity

Look at a map of Japan and pick out a city. Look up a weather report in a newspaper or on the Internet (you can go to *www.weather.com*). Find out what the weather is like in the city you chose in Japan. For older students, try locating a city on each one of the four major islands.

Tokyo

Tokyo is the capital of Japan. In the center of the city is the ancient Imperial Palace. The royal family of Japan, the emperor and his family, live there today.

Some ancient buildings in Tokyo in the traditional style are called *pagodas* (pah-GOH-dahs). They are wooden structures

with roofs that curve up at the ends. They were built as memorials or shrines. The modern buildings are made of glass and steel and tower many stories high. The business districts of Tokyo have row after row of tall skyscrapers.

Tokyo has one of the fastest trains in the world, called *Shinkansen* (sheen-KAHN-sehn). It travels over 130 mph (209 km/h). It is more comfortable than the commuter trains, but it is very expensive.

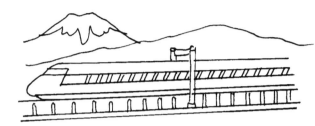

Activity

Invite someone who has visited or lived in Japan to be a guest speaker in the classroom. Ask if they could bring photographs or slides of their trip. Then discuss with the students what they would most like to do in Japan: go shopping or sight-seeing in Tokyo, visit a famous shrine or temple, climb Mount Fuji, see a Kabuki or Bunraku play, or attend a tea ceremony in a Japanese garden.

Activity

Explore *www.artisandevelopers.com/web/ tokyo*. This is a guided tour through Tokyo by some tourists who took the time to capture many of Tokyo's highlights. It has a musical background, informational and educational links, and lots of great pictures. It also contains Tokyo's current time.

Activity

Read *The Park Bench* by Fumiko Takeshita, a book about present-day Japan.

Activity

Help students complete the map activity on page 45.

Samurai Maze

Help this samurai get to Edo Castle.

START

FINISH

Map Activity

Hokkaido

Sea of Japan

Pacific Ocean

Kyoto

Honshu

Hiroshima

Mt. Fuji

Tokyo

Osaka

Kyushu → Shikoku

1. Color the Pacific Ocean blue.

2. Color the Sea of Japan light blue.

3. Find Tokyo and draw a star where it is located.

4. Draw a mountain where Mount Fuji is.

5. Color the island of Hokkaido orange.

6. Color the island of Honshu red.

7. Color the island of Shikoku green.

8. Color the island of Kyushu brown.

45

Instructions:

Enlarge to 200%. Fold on the dotted line. Then glue the sides of the suitcase, leaving the top open. (You may wish to glue the suitcase to a file folder for added stability.) Punch out the circles with a hole punch and thread yarn or string through the holes. Knot the thread for handles.

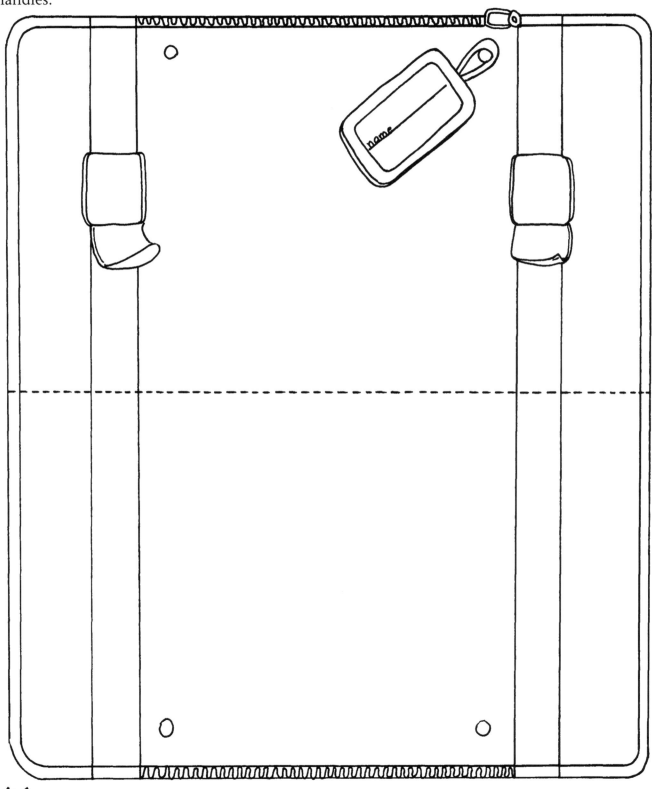

46

References

Bibliography and Photographic Reference

Collcutt, Martin, Marius Jansen, and Isao Kumakura. *Cultural Atlas of Japan.* New York: Facts on File, 1988.

Doran, Clare. *The Japanese.* New York: Thomson Learning, 1995.

Galvin, Irene Flum. *Japan: A Modern World with Ancient Roots.* New York: Benchmark Books, 1996.

Kent, Deborah. *Cities of the World: Tokyo.* New York: Children's Press, 1996.

National Council for Social Studies. *Tora no Maki II.* Washington, D.C., National Council for the Social Studies/Social Science Education, 1997.

Ridgwell, Jenny. *A Taste of Japan.* New York: Thomson Learning, 1997.

Scoones, Simon. *A Family from Japan.* Austin, TX: Raintree Steck-Vaughn Publishers, 1998.

Shelley, Rex. *Cultures of the World: Japan.* New York: Marshall Cavendish, 1990.

Streissguth, Tom. *Globe-Trotters Club: Japan.* Minneapolis: Carolrhoda Books, 1997.

—A *Ticket to Japan.* Minneapolis: Carolrhoda Books, 1997.

Children's Literature Reference

Ashley, Bernard. *Cleversticks.* New York: Random House, 1995.

Brenner, Barbara, and Julia Takaya. *Chibi: A True Story from Japan.* New York: Clarion Books, 1996.

Cobb, Vicki. *This Place Is Crowded: Japan.* New York: Walker and Company, 1992.

Coerr, Eleanor. *Mieko and the Fifth Treasure.* New York: G. P. Putnam's Sons, 1993.

—*Sadako and the Thousand Paper Cranes.* New York: Dell Publishing, 1977.

Dooley, Norah. *Everybody Cooks Rice.* Minneapolis: Carolrhoda Books, 1991.

Friedman, Ina R. *How My Parents Learned to Eat.* Boston: Houghton Mifflin, 1984.

Hidaka, Masako. *Girl from the Snow Country.* Translated by Amanda Mayer Stinchecum. Brooklyn: Kane/Miller, 1986.

Hughes, Monica. *Little Fingerling: A Japanese Folktale.* Nashville: Ideals Children's Books, 1992.

Kalman, Maira. *Sayonara, Mrs. Kackleman.* New York: Puffin, 1991.

Levine, Arthur A. *The Boy Who Drew Cats: A Japanese Folktale.* New York: Dial Books for Young Readers, 1994.

Long, Jan Freeman. *The Bee and the Dream: A Japanese Tale.* New York: Dutton Children's Books, 1996.

Merrill, Jean. *The Girl Who Loved Caterpillars: A Twelfth Century Tale from Japan.* New York: Philomel Books, 1992.

References

Nakawatari, Harutaka. *The Sea and I.* Translated by Susan Matsui. New York: Farrar, Straus & Giroux, 1994.

Paterson, Katherine. *The Tale of the Mandarin Ducks.* New York: Puffin, 1995.

Say, Allen. *Tree of Cranes.* Boston: Houghton Mifflin, 1991.

Normura, Takaaki. *Grandpa's Town.* Translated by Amanda M. Stinchecum. Brooklyn: Kane/Miller, 1991.

Takeshita, Fumiko. *The Park Bench.* Translated by Ruth A. Kanagy. Brooklyn: Kane/Miller, 1988.

Wells, Rosemary. *Yoko.* New York: Hyperion Books for Children, 1998.

Web Site Reference
(The date in parentheses represents the last date the Web site was checked by the publisher.)

Speaking Japanese

"Kanji Names Project: List of Names," 27 January, 1999, <http://www2.gol.com/users/billp/students/kanjiname/nameindex.html> (17 February, 2000).

Steve Fylypchuk, "Ste-Chan's Kanji of the Day," 21 January, 1998. <http://www.globalserve.net/~fylypchuk/kanji/kanjiframe.html> (17 February, 2000).

Japanese Arts

Matthew Johnson, "Kabuki for Everyone," <http://www.fix.co.jp/kabuki/kabuki.html> (17 February, 2000).

Temples and Shrines

International Association of Japanese Gardens, Inc., Homepage, <http://www.japanese-gardens-assoc.org> (17 February, 2000).

History and Geography

"Welcome to Edo," <http://www.us-japan.org/edomatsu> (17 February, 2000)

Roger and Marilyn Jesrani, "Welcome to Roger & Marilyn's Photo Tour of Tokyo, Japan," <http://www.artisandevelopers.com/web/tokyo> (17 February, 2000).

The Weather Channel Enterprises, Inc., Homepage, <http://www.weather.com> (17 February, 2000).